Physical Science
Laboratory Manual

by
Robert Marshall
and
Donald H. Jacobs

AGS®
American Guidance Service, Inc.
Circle Pines, Minnesota 55014-1796
800-328-2560

Printed in the United States of America

ISBN 0-7854-1021-X

Product Number 90294

A 0 9 8 7 6 5

Table of Contents

Name Date Period

Safety in the Science Laboratory

General Rules

1. Clean area free of unneeded objects.
2. Do not play in the laboratory.
3. Keep equipment in good working order.

Heat

1. Be aware of all open flames. Flames are difficult to see on Bunsen burners.
2. Never touch flames.
3. Never touch the surface of the hotplate.
4. When heating chemicals, point test tubes away from any people.

Electricity

1. Never use household current without proper supervision.
2. Remember that electricity flowing in wires causes the wires to become hot. Do not burn yourself.

Chemicals

1. Never smell chemicals directly.
2. Never taste unknown chemicals.
3. Remember that even the simplest of chemicals can cause hazardous reactions.
4. Always do chemical tests under adult supervision.
5. Do not place your fingers in your mouth while working with chemicals.
6. Always wash your hands after working with chemicals.

Name Date Period

Some Common Science Equipment

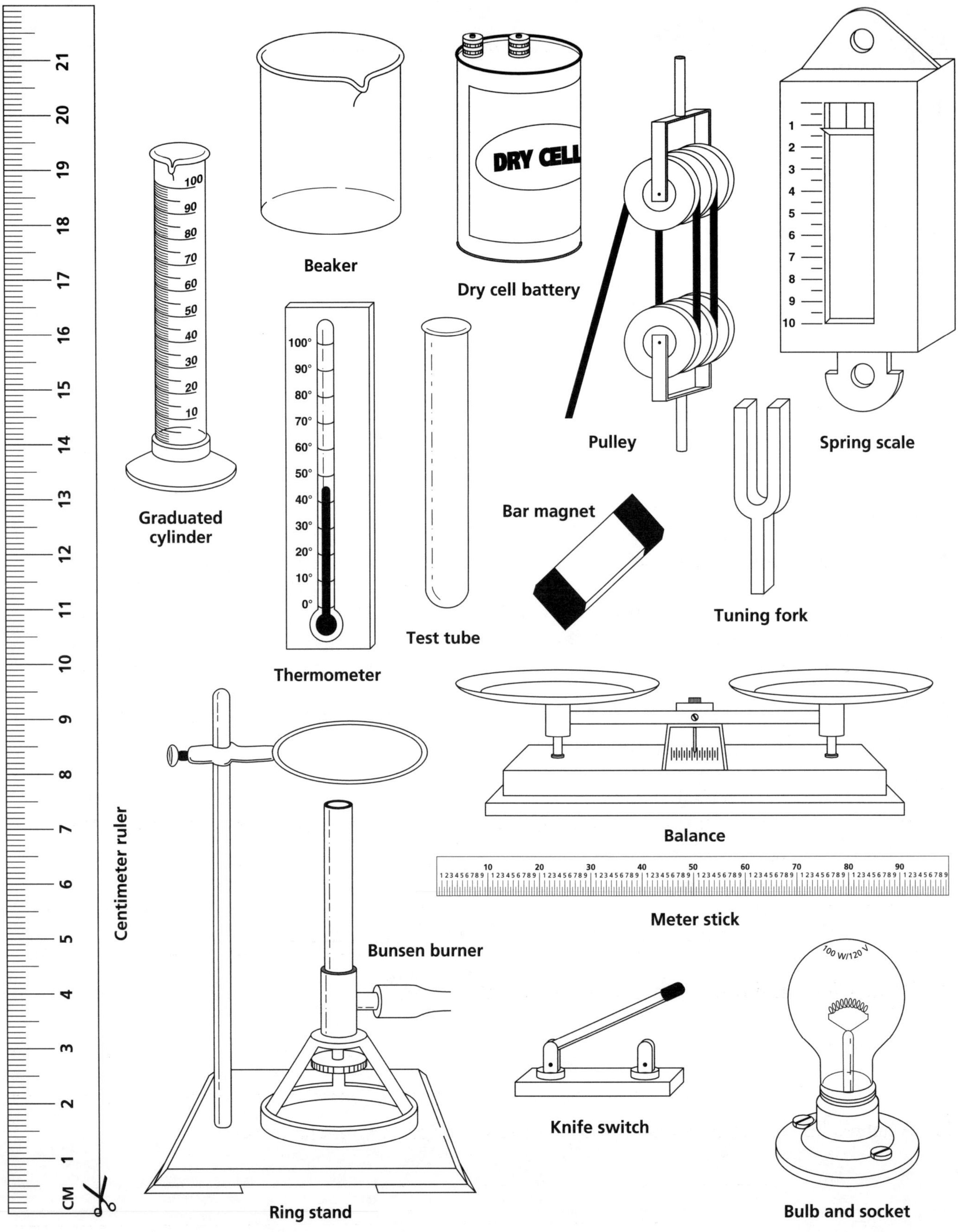

Name Date Period

Safety in the Classroom

Purpose: To identify and locate safety equipment in the classroom

Materials: meter stick
metric ruler
colored pencil

Procedure

1. With a partner, draw a floor diagram of your classroom. Use the grid on the next page to make your diagram. Draw your diagram as close to the actual scale as possible. Include the location of desks, windows, doors, cabinets, and any other large items.
2. Survey your classroom for safety equipment, such as fire extinguishers and safety goggles. On your diagram, mark the location of the safety equipment. Use a different symbol for each piece of equipment. In one corner of your diagram, make a key for the symbols you use.
3. Locate the electrical outlets in the classroom. On your diagram, use symbols to mark the location of the outlets. Include the symbols in the key.
4. If your classroom has gas outlets, use a symbol to mark these on the diagram. Include the symbol in the key.
5. Mark the location of your work station. Use a colored pencil to map out the quickest and safest route for you to exit the classroom in case of an emergency.
6. On your diagram, mark any other information that you think is important.

Questions

1. Suppose the route you marked for a safe exit from the classroom becomes blocked. What other route might you take?

____

____

2. What safety equipment is available in your classroom?

____

____

3. What additional equipment would you like included in your classroom?

____

Safety in the Classroom, continued

Name Date Period

1-1 Hands Instead of Feet

Use with Investigation 1-1, pages 12–13

Purpose: To create a system of measuring length and to compare it to the metric system

Object	Length in hands	Length in centimeters

Questions

1. Did your length in hands match those of other students? Why or why not?

2. Did your length in centimeters match those of other students? Why or why not?

3. Do you think a system such as the metric system is more useful than one that uses units such as hands? Explain.

1-2 Counting Squares and Calculating Area

Use with Investigation 1-2, pages 16–17

Purpose: To understand the relationship between area and the number of square units

	Length	Width	Area (length × width)	Total number of squares
original paper				
rectangle 1				
rectangle 2				

Questions

1. Did the area you found for the original paper in step 5 match the area calculated in step 2? Do you think it should? Explain.

2. How did the sum of the areas of the two new rectangles compare to the total number of squares in the two rectangles? How did it compare to the calculated area of the original sheet of paper? Explain these results.

Name Date Period

Chapter 1 Lab Manual 4

Finding Volume

Purpose: To measure objects and to calculate their volume

Materials: metric ruler
various rectangular boxes, such as cereal box, CD box, toothpaste box, pizza box, shoe box, film box

Procedure

1. Use the table below to record your data.

	Kind of box	Length	Height	Width	Volume (L × W × H)
1					
2					
3					
4					
5					
6					

2. Observe the boxes you are going to measure. Which one do you think has the largest volume?

____

3. Choose one of the boxes. Write a description of the box in the data table.
4. Measure the length, width, and height of one of the boxes. Measure in millimeters or centimeters. Record the measurements in the first row of the data table.
5. Multiply the length by the width. Then multiply that answer by the height. The result is the volume of the box. The volume will be in cubic millimeters or cubic centimeters. Write the volume in the data table in the last column of the row.
6. Repeat steps 3 and 5 with the other boxes.

Finding Volume, continued

Questions

1. Which box had the greatest length?

____

The greatest width?

____

The greatest height?

____

2. Which box had the largest volume?

____

3. Did you correctly predict which box had the largest volume?

____

4. Which box had the smallest volume?

____

5. Do you think it is easy to predict the volume of an object just by looking at it? Explain.

____

____

Explore Further

Arrange your boxes according to height, from tallest to shortest. Then arrange them according to volume, from greatest to smallest. Which boxes are in new positions?

Name ____________________ Date __________ Period __________

2-1 Identifying Properties

Use with Investigation 2-1, pages 30–31

Purpose: To write clear descriptions of objects

Object number	Properties
1	
2	
3	
4	
5	

Questions

1. How many objects did your classmate identify correctly?

____

2. What could you have done to make your descriptions more useful?

____

____

____

____

____

Name Date Period

Measuring Mass

Purpose: To measure the mass of various objects

Materials: balance
standard masses
penny
nickel
dime
quarter
pen
pencil
2 other small objects

Procedure

1. Use the table below to record your data.

Object	Estimated mass (g)	Measured mass (g)
penny		
nickel		
dime		
quarter		
pen		
pencil		

2. Estimate the mass of the penny. Record your estimate in the table.
3. Place the penny in one of the pans on the balance.
4. Place standard masses in the other pan until the two sides balance. Add the masses of the standard masses to find the mass of the penny. Record this mass in the first row of the data table.
5. Repeat steps 2–4, using the other objects. Then repeat the procedure, using two objects of your choice.

Measuring Mass, continued

Questions

1. Which object had the most mass?

____

2. Which object had the least mass?

____

3. Which has more mass, the penny or the nickel?

____

4. Which would have more mass, two pennies or the nickel?

____

5. How did the actual measured masses compare to your estimated masses?

____

____

Name Date Period

Measuring Volume

Purpose: To find the volume of various objects

Materials: cap from tube of toothpaste
graduated cylinder
paper towels
cap from mouthwash bottle
penny
marble
stone
game die
metric ruler

Procedure

1. Use the table below to record your data.

Object	Estimated volume (mL)	Measured volume (mL)
toothpaste cap		
mouthwash cap		
penny		
marble		
stone		
game die—using displacement of water		
game die—using a formula		

2. Estimate the volume in milliliters of each object in the table. Record your estimates in the data table.
3. Fill the toothpaste cap with water. Then pour the water into a dry graduated cylinder.
4. Read the volume of the water from the scale on the graduated cylinder. (If you need help reading a scale, use page 38 of your text.) Record the volume of the water in the table. Use a paper towel to dry the cylinder.
5. Repeat steps 3 and 4, using the mouthwash cap.

Measuring Volume, continued

6. Measure the volume of the penny, marble, stone, and game die. Use the displacement of water method described on page 41 of your text. Record these volumes in the table.
7. Use the metric ruler to measure the length, width, and height of the game die. Find the volume of the die. To find the volume, use the formula: length × width × height. Record the volume of the die in the table.

Questions

1. Which object has the largest volume?

____

2. List the objects in order from smallest volume to largest volume.

____

3. You measured the volume of the game die, using two different methods. Do your volumes agree?

____

4. How do your predictions about the volume of the objects compare to the measured volumes?

____

5. Suppose you wanted to find the volume of a cup that had a volume greater than the graduated cylinder. How could you measure the cup's volume without using additional materials?

____

____

____

2-2 Finding Density

Use with Investigation 2-2, pages 45–46

Purpose: To calculate and compare the densities of oil and water

	Cylinder with water	Cylinder with oil
A. mass of empty cylinder		
B. mass of cylinder and liquid		
C. mass of liquid (B – A)		
D. volume of liquid		
E. density $\left(E = \frac{C}{D}\right)$		

Questions

1. Which substance—the water or the oil—has the greater density?

____

____

2. Liquids with lesser densities will float on liquids with greater densities. If you pour oil and water together, which liquid would float on top?

____

____

3-1 Breaking Down Water

Use with Investigation 3-1, pages 62–63

Purpose: To show that water is made from two different substances and is therefore a compound

	After 10 minutes
Wire connected to positive (+) terminal	
Wire connected to negative (–) terminal	

Questions

1. Which of the wires had more bubbles around it? Identify the wire by telling whether it was connected to the positive (+) terminal or the negative (–) terminal.

____

2. Describe what you observed at the end of each wire after 10 minutes.

____

____

3. The gas you observe comes from the water. The electricity from the batteries breaks down the water into hydrogen gas and oxygen gas. How does this production of gases show that water is a compound?

____

____

____

Inferring the Properties of an Object

Purpose: To infer the properties of a hidden object

Materials: clay
plastic knife
small object, such as a short piece of chalk, pencil eraser, or coin
paper clip

Procedure

1. Use the table below to record your observations.

	What I think the object is like	What the object actually is like
size		
shape		
hardness		
position		
other		

2. Make a clay "atom." Form the clay into a large ball. Cut the ball in half with the plastic knife. Place a small object between the halves, and smooth them together. Your object should now be hidden inside the clay ball.

3. Exchange clay "atoms" with a partner.

4. Unbend the paper clip until it is fairly straight.

5. Carefully insert the paper clip into your partner's clay ball to help you get information about the object that is hidden in the ball. Some properties of the object that you should try to find out are size, shape, hardness, and position in the clay.

Inferring the Properties of an Object, continued

6. Repeat step 5 as many times as you need to. Fill in the first column of the data table as you gather information.
7. When you have gathered as much information as possible, make a drawing on another sheet of paper showing what you think the clay "atom" looks like inside.
8. Carefully cut the clay ball open to reveal the object. Fill in the second column of the table.

Questions

1. Were you able to infer the correct size of the object?

____

2. Were you able to infer the correct shape of the object?

____

3. Were you able to infer the correct hardness of the object?

____

4. Were you able to infer the correct position of the object?

____

5. Which property was the easiest to infer?

____

6. Which property was the hardest to infer?

____

7. How is this activity similar to the method scientists use to develop models of atoms?

____

____

____

____

3-2 Making Models of Atoms

Use with Investigation 3-2, pages 68–69

Purpose: To make a model of an atom of a particular element

Name of element
Picture of element

Questions

1. What is the name of your element? How many protons are in the nucleus? How many neutrons?

____

2. How many electrons does your element have?

____

3. Write at least four things that your model shows about atoms.

____

____

____

____

____

Exploring the Space Between Particles

Purpose: To observe that there is space between particles

Materials: three 250-mL beakers
marbles
sand
water

Procedure

1. Use the table below to record your data.

	Volume (mL)		
	Beaker A	**Beaker B**	**Beaker C**
at start of experiment			
after adding sand to beaker A			
after adding water to beaker A			

2. Label the beakers *A, B,* and *C.*

3. Fill beaker A with marbles to the 200-mL line. Do not let any marbles go above the 200-mL mark. Record in the data table the volume of the marbles.

4. Fill beaker B with sand to the 200-mL line. Record the volume.

5. Fill beaker C with water to the 200-mL line. Record the volume.

6. Pour some sand from beaker B into beaker A. Pour the sand to the 200-mL mark. Do not let any sand go above the 200-mL mark. Fill in the second row of the data table.

7. Pour water from beaker C into beaker A. Pour the water to the 200-mL mark. Do not let any water go above the 200-mL line. Fill in the third row of the data table.

Exploring the Space Between Particles, continued

Questions

1. What was the volume of marbles before you added sand or water to the beaker?

2. Did the marbles fill all of this space? How do you know?

3. What was the total volume of sand that you added to the beaker of marbles. (*Hint:* Subtract the volume of sand in beaker B after you added the sand to beaker A from the volume of sand before you added it.)

4. What was the total volume of water that you added to the beaker of marbles. (*Hint:* Subtract the volume of water in beaker C after you added the water to beaker A from the volume of water before you added it.)

5. What was the total volume of sand and water added to the marbles? (*Hint:* Add the volumes from questions 3 and 4.)

6. What is the volume of space that was present between the marbles before you added anything to the beaker? How do you know?

7. How does this activity help you understand the model of an atom?

Name Date Period

4-1 Finding Iron in Your Cereal

Use with Investigation 4-1, pages 82–83

Purpose: To observe bits of iron in an iron-fortified cereal

Procedure step	Observations
7	
8	
9	

Questions

1. What did you observe on the end of the magnet?

____

2. What did you observe on the white paper?

____

3. Were the bits on the white paper attracted to the magnet?

____

4. What element from the cereal did you see?

____

Name Date Period

Analyzing Common Compounds

Purpose: To determine what elements make up various household chemicals

Materials: safety goggles, hand lens, salt, baking soda, sugar, water, nail polish remover, vinegar

Procedure

1. Use the table below to record your observations.

Compound	Chemical name	Chemical formula	Observations
salt	sodium chloride	$NaCl$	
baking soda	sodium bicarbonate	$NaHCO_3$	
sugar	sucrose	$C_6H_{12}O_2$	
water	hydrogen oxide	H_2O	
nail polish remover	acetone	CH_3COCH_3	
vinegar	acetic acid hydrate	$HC_2H_3O_2$	

2. Put on your safety goggles.
3. Carefully observe a small amount of the salt. Record in the data table your observations about the salt.
4. Repeat step 3 for the remaining materials. *Safety Alert: Do not breathe in the nail polish remover. Do not taste any of the materials.*

Analyzing Common Compounds, continued

Questions

1. The chemical formula of a compound shows the symbols of the elements that are in the compound. What elements are in each of the compounds?

   salt ______

   baking soda ______

   sugar ______

   water ______

   nail polish remover ______

   vinegar ______

2. Which compound has the most different elements?

   ______

3. Which compounds contain carbon?

   ______

4. Which element is present in all the compounds?

   ______

5. Sugar and nail polish remover are made of the same three elements—carbon, hydrogen, and oxygen. Do these two substances have similar properties?

   ______

   ______

   ______

6. Why do you think sugar and nail polish remover are so different yet are made of the same elements?

   ______

   ______

   ______

Name Date Period

Exploring Elements

Purpose: To classify a group of elements

Materials: encyclopedia or other reference materials
index cards

Procedure

1. Use the table below to record information.

Element	Atomic number	Atomic mass	State (solid, liquid, or gas)	Color	Density (g/cm^3)

2. Work in a group with four other students. Each student should choose five elements to research. Make sure no two group members choose the same element.

3. Research your five elements. Write in the data table the information you find about your elements.

4. Make an index card for each of your elements. Write the information from the data table on the card. Include any other information you think is important or interesting.

5. Gather all 25 cards from your group. See how many different ways you can classify the elements.

6. Choose one classification system that your group thinks is best.

Exploring Elements, continued

Questions

1. How many ways did you find to classify the elements?

2. Did some ways work better than others? Why?

3. Which classification system did your group think best? According to which properties were the cards in this classification system grouped?

4. How could you make your classification system better?

Explore Further

Work with three other groups of five students to research the first 100 elements. Can you classify them the way you classified your 25 elements? Can you classify them the way any of the other groups classified their 25 elements? Are there any other ways you can classify elements?

4-2 Electricity and Metals

Use with Investigation 4-2, pages 97–98

Purpose: To determine which materials carry electricity

	Observations
copper wires	
sulfur	
aluminum	

Questions

1. What happened to the light bulb when you held the copper wires together?

2. What happened to the light bulb when you held the samples of sulfur and aluminum between the wires?

3. What did you observe about the ability of copper, sulfur, and aluminum to carry electricity?

4. Which materials do you think are metals? Why?

5-1 Observing a Chemical Change

Use with Investigation 5-1, pages 106–107

Purpose: To observe physical and chemical changes

	Appearance
washing soda in water	
Epsom salts in water	
washing soda and Epsom salts in water	

Questions

1. What happened when you added the washing soda to water?

2. What happened when you added the Epsom salts to water?

3. What did you observe when you mixed the contents of the jars together in step 6?

4. Did a chemical change or a physical change take place in steps 4 and 5? Explain your answer.

5. Did a chemical change or a physical change take place in step 6? Explain your answer.

Observing a Chemical Reaction

Purpose: To observe the reaction of several compounds

Materials:
safety goggles
calcium chloride (CaCl)
baking soda ($NaHCO_3$)
spoon
locking plastic bag
small paper cup
water (H_2O)
graduated cylinder
paper towel

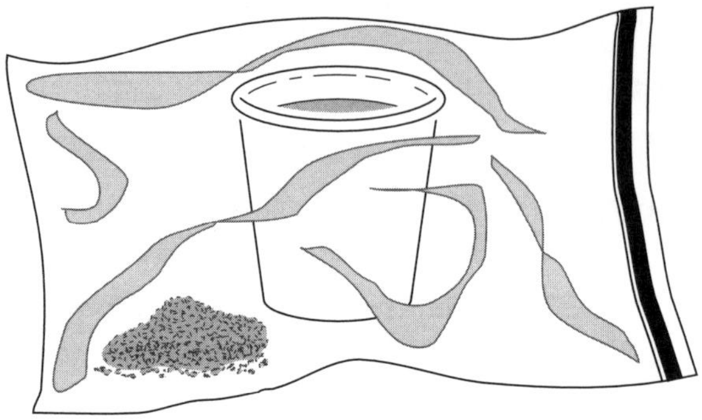

Procedure

1. Use the table below to record your data.

	Description of plastic bag
before adding water	
after adding water	

2. Put on your safety goggles.

3. Place 2 spoonfuls of calcium chloride in the plastic bag.

4. Add 2 spoonfuls of baking soda to the calcium chloride in the plastic bag. Seal the bag. Shake it to mix the materials.

5. Use the graduated cylinder to measure 50 mL of water.

6. Pour the 50 mL of water into the paper cup. Wipe off the outside and the bottom of the cup with the paper towel. Open the plastic bag and carefully put the cup inside. Make sure that none of the powder gets wet. Seal the plastic bag.

Observing a Chemical Reaction, continued

7. Observe the contents of the bag. Record your observations in the first row of the data table.
8. Tip over the cup to spill the water into the bag. Make sure the powder gets wet. Write your observations in the second row of the data table.

Questions

1. What materials did you put into the bag? Were they elements or compounds?

___

___

___

2. How did the contents of the bag change after you spilled the water?

___

___

3. Did a chemical reaction occur when you mixed the calcium chloride and the baking soda? How do you know?

___

___

___

4. Did a chemical reaction occur when you mixed the water with the calcium chloride and the baking soda? How do you know?

___

___

___

5-2 Identifying Acids and Bases

Use with Investigation 5-2, pages 125–126

Purpose: To use an indicator to test for acids and bases

Substance	**Color after cabbage juice is added**	**Acid or base**
baking soda		base
vinegar		acid
lemon juice		
weak ammonia		
aspirin		
soap		
soft drink		
milk of magnesia		

Questions

1. Which of the substances are acids?

____

____

2. Which of the substances are bases?

____

____

3. Are some bases stronger than others? Explain your answer.

____

____

____

____

____

____

Exploring Acidity

Purpose: To determine the effects that acids and bases have on litmus paper

Materials:

- safety goggles
- salt
- spoon
- drinking straw
- orange juice
- dish-washing liquid
- red litmus paper
- 6 small paper cups
- water
- vinegar
- milk
- antacid liquid
- blue litmus paper

Procedure

1. Use the table below to record your data.

Acid or Base Pre-diction	Item	Effect on red litmus paper	Effect on blue litmus paper
	salt water		
	vinegar		
	orange juice		
	milk		
	dish-washing liquid		
	antacid liquid		

2. Put on your safety goggles.

3. Pour 1 spoonful of salt into a paper cup and fill the cup with water. Stir the mixture with the plastic straw to dissolve the salt.

4. Pour into separate paper cups a small amount of each of the remaining materials listed in the data table.

5. Take one of the sample cups. Dip a strip of red litmus paper and a strip of blue litmus paper into the sample. Hold the strips in the sample for 30 seconds. Then remove the strips. Write your observations in the data table.

6. Repeat step 5 for the remaining sample cups.

Exploring Acidity, continued

Questions

1. Did the orange juice affect the red litmus paper? If so, how?

2. Did the orange juice affect the blue litmus paper? If so, how?

3. Orange juice and vinegar are acids. How do acids affect red litmus paper?

4. How do acids affect blue litmus paper?

5. Dish-washing liquid and antacid liquid are bases. How do bases affect red litmus paper?

6. How do bases affect blue litmus paper?

7. Salt water and milk are not acids or bases. How do they affect red litmus paper?

8. How do substances that are not acids or bases affect blue litmus paper?

9. How can you use litmus paper to test for acids and bases?

6-1

Separating a Mixture

Use with Investigation 6-1, pages 134–135

Purpose: To use dissolving to separate a mixture

	Observations
salt	
sand	
mixture of salt and sand	
solution of salt, sand, and water	
filter paper	
sides of beaker	

Questions

1. In steps 5 and 6, what happens to the salt when the water is added to the mixture?

2. In step 6, does the sand dissolve? How do you know?

3. In step 8, where is the salt after you pour the solution into the second beaker? How do you know?

4. In step 9, which material remains on the filter paper? How do you know?

5. In step 11, what substance forms on the side of the beaker?

6. What is the solvent in this Investigation? ______

7. What is the solute? ______

Speed of Dissolving

Purpose: To observe what factors affect the speed with which sugar will dissolve

Materials: 4 beakers
water
4 sugar cubes
metal spoon
paper towel
clock with second hand

Procedure

1. Use the table below to record your data.

	Dissolving Time	
	Crushed sugar cube	**Whole sugar cube**
stirred		
not stirred		

2. Fill each of the beakers with 100 mL of water.

3. Wrap one of the sugar cubes in a paper towel. Use the spoon to crush the sugar cubes into granules.

4. Pour the granules into one of the beakers of water. Stir with the spoon. Time how long it takes the granules to dissolve. Write the information in the data table.

5. Drop a whole sugar cube into another beaker of water. Stir. Time how long it takes the cube to dissolve. Write the information in the data table.

6. Repeat steps 3–5, but do not stir. (You may want to set a 5-minute time limit for each step.)

Speed of Dissolving, continued

Questions

1. In which beaker did the sugar dissolve faster—in the beaker with crushed sugar or in the beaker with the whole sugar cube?

____

2. The figures below show two sugar cubes. One cube is whole. The other cube is broken into eight pieces. Use the figures to explain your answer to question 1.

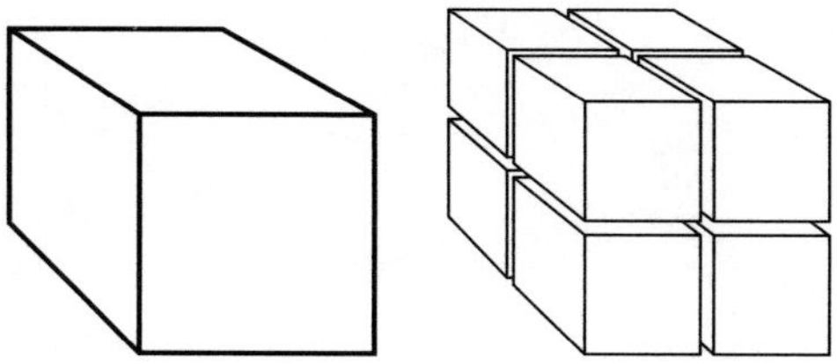

____

____

____

____

3. Did stirring affect the speed of dissolving? If so, how?

____

____

4. Many food products, such as instant tea and coffee, come in powdered form. Why do you think this is so?

____

____

____

Temperature and Chemical Reactions

Purpose: To determine how temperature affects the speed of a chemical reaction

Materials: safety goggles
2 balloons
2 one-hole rubber stoppers
2 flasks
250 mL hot water
250 mL cold water
4 antacid tablets
clock with second hand

Procedure

1. Use the table below to record your data.

Time	Flask A (hot water)	Flask B (cold water)
beginning		
20 seconds		
40 seconds		
1 minute		
1 minute 20 seconds		
1 minute 40 seconds		
2 minutes		
2 minutes 20 seconds		
2 minutes 40 seconds		
3 minutes		

2. Read the entire procedure several times before beginning. Steps 8 and 9 will happen very quickly. Be sure you know what to do.

3. Work with a partner. One of you should be the timer. The other will be the recorder.

4. Label the flasks *A* and *B*.

Temperature and Chemical Reactions, continued

5. Put on your safety goggles.
6. Stretch the mouth of each balloon around a rubber stopper. Make sure that the stoppers will still fit in the flasks after you attach the balloons.
7. Fill flask A with 250 mL of hot water. Fill flask B with 250 mL of cold water.
8. Place one flask in front of you and the other flask in front of your partner. Hold a stopper in one hand and 2 antacid tablets in the other hand. Have your partner do the same. At exactly the same time, both of you should drop the tablets in the water and immediately put the stopper in the flask. Make sure the stoppers fit tightly.
9. As soon as the stoppers are in the flasks, the timer begins to time the experiment. Every 20 seconds, the timer says, "Now." When the timer says, "Now," the recorder writes down how full each balloon is. The timer may scribble notes quickly on a sheet of paper and later copy the notes onto the data table.

Questions

1. Did a chemical reaction occur in either of the flasks? How do you know?

____

____

____

2. Did water temperature affect what happened? If so, how?

____

____

____

3. How does heat affect the speed of a chemical reaction?

____

____

____

Name Date Period

6-2 Observing Different Kinds of Reactions

Use with Investigation 6-2, pages 147–148

Purpose: To study the four main types of chemical reactions

Reaction	Observations
1	
2	
3	
4	

Questions

Complete the following table.

Reaction	Equation	Type of reaction
1	$4Fe + 3O_2 \rightarrow 2Fe_2O_3$	
2	$2H_2O_2 \rightarrow 2H_2O + O_2$	
3	$Fe + CuSO_4 \rightarrow FeSO_4 + Cu$	
4	$Na_2CO_3 + CaCl_2 \rightarrow NaCl + CaCO_3$	

7-1 Finding Speed

Use with Investigation 7-1, pages 164–165

Purpose: To calculate speed by measuring distance and time, and to use a graph to show motion

Length (meters)	Time (seconds)	Speed (distance/time)

Questions

1. Make a graph with distance in meters on the vertical (up-and-down) axis. Place time in seconds on the horizontal (left-to-right) axis. Extend the axes twice as far as you need to in order to graph your data. Plot one point where 0 seconds crosses 0 meters, to show the beginning of the roll. Plot a second point, using the distance and time values you recorded. Connect the two points with a straight line.

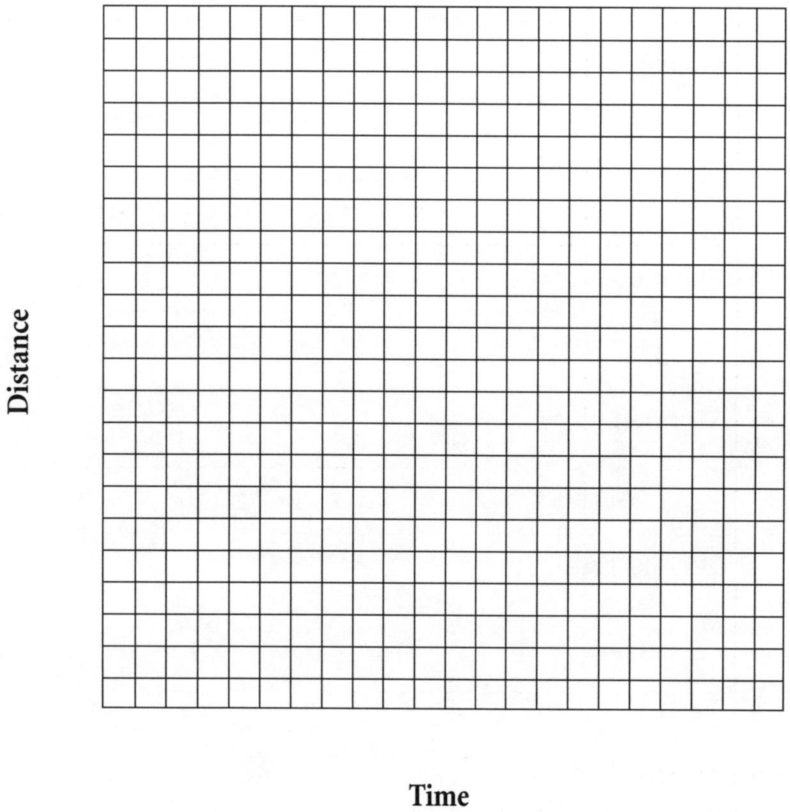

2. Use the graph you made to estimate the distance the ball traveled after it had been moving for half the recorded time.

____

3. Extend the graph. Estimate the distance the ball would have gone if it had traveled for twice the recorded time.

____

Name Date Period

Chapter 7
Lab Manual 26

Exploring Acceleration

Purpose: To examine changes in speed and direction

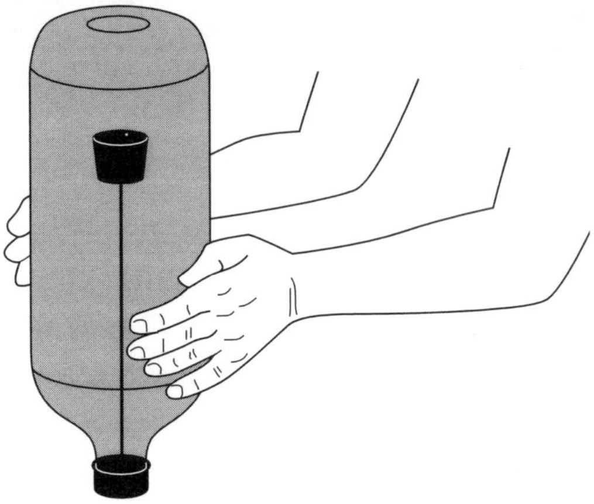

Materials: safety goggles
cork
needle
piece of thread, 20 cm long
2-L plastic soft-drink bottle with cap
masking tape
water

Procedure

1. Use the table below to record your data.

Change in motion	How I think the cork will move	How the cork moved
started		
stopped		
turned right		
turned left		

2. Put on your safety goggles.

3. Insert the needle into the cork.

4. Thread the string through one end of the needle and tie it. Tape the other end of the thread to the inside of the bottle top, as shown in the figure above.

5. Fill the bottle with water.

6. Lower the cork into the bottle. Place the top on the bottle. Make sure all the thread is inside the bottle. Screw the bottle cap on tightly.

Exploring Acceleration, continued

7. Look at the motions described in the first column of the data table. How do you think the cork will move if you carry the bottle upside down and perform each of the movements? Write your predictions in the second column of the data table.
8. Carefully turn the bottle upside down.
9. Hold the bottle at arm's length so you can easily see the cork. Move around the room, changing your speed and direction quickly. For example, start walking quickly. Next, stop walking quickly. Walk forward, then suddenly step to the left. Each time you change your motion, observe the cork. Write your observations in the data table.

Questions

1. When you suddenly moved forward, what did the cork do?

____

____

2. When you moved forward and then stopped, what did the cork do?

____

____

3. When you turned right, what did the cork do?

____

____

4. When you turned left, what did the cork do?

____

____

Newton's First Law of Motion

Purpose: To observe the first law of motion

Materials: shoe box
scissors
tennis ball
index card
quarter

Procedure

1. Use the table below to record your data.

	Observations
tennis ball	
quarter	

2. Cut one end from the side of the shoe box, as shown in the figure below.

3. Place the shoe box on the floor with the open end pointing toward a wall. Place the tennis ball inside the box opposite the opening you made.

4. Rapidly push the box toward the wall. Then stop the box suddenly. Observe what happens to the ball. Write your observations in the data table.

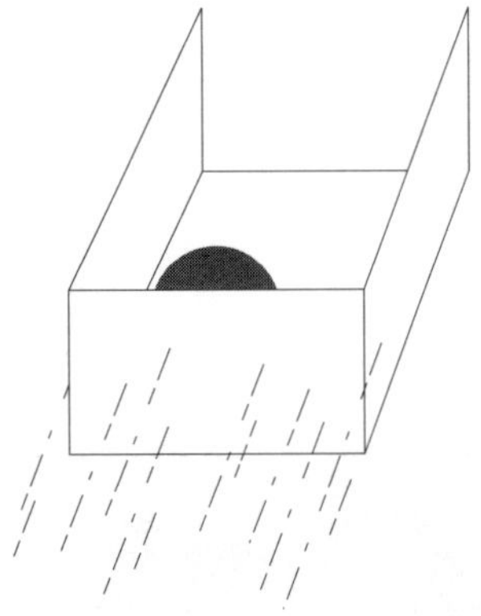

Newton's First Law of Motion, continued

5. Place the index card on the edge of a table. Make sure some of it extends over the edge of the table.

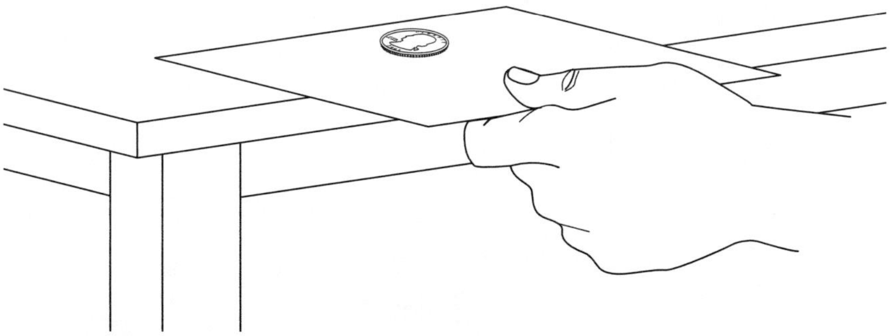

6. Place the quarter on the index card.
7. Quickly pull the index card straight out from the table. Observe what happens to the quarter. Write your observations in the data table.

Questions

1. In step 4, when you started moving the box, what happened to the ball?

____

2. In step 4, when you stopped pushing the box, what happened to the ball?

____

3. When you placed the quarter on the index card, neither the card nor the quarter was moving. What happened when you moved the index card?

____

4. Explain how this activity demonstrates Newton's first law of motion

____

____

____

____

____

7-2 Newton's Third Law of Motion

Use with Investigation 7-2, pages 175–176

Purpose: To demonstrate action and reaction

Observations	
Part A	**Part B**

Questions

1. In Part A, in what direction does the escaping air move?

____

2. In Part A, in what direction does the balloon move?

____

3. How does Part A demonstrate Newton's third law of motion?

____

____

____

4. In Part B, in what direction does the balloon move?

____

5. In Part B, in what direction does the ball move?

____

6. In Part B, use Newton's third law of motion to explain why the ball moves the way it does.

____

____

Name Date Period

8-1 Mass, Height, and Energy

Use with Investigation 8-1, pages 190–191

Purpose: To demonstrate how mass affects potential and kinetic energy

Object	Distance cup moved
small marble	
large marble	
small marble	
large marble	

Questions

1. Which marble pushed the cup farther from the ramp?

____

____

2. What conclusion can you draw about the effect of mass on kinetic energy?

____

____

____

____

8-2 Finding the Mechanical Advantage of a Lever

Use with Investigation 8-2, pages 200–201

Purpose: To find the mechanical advantage of levers

Fulcrum position	Resistance force	Effort force	Resistance arm	Effort arm
50 cm				
80 cm				
20 cm				

Questions

1. Where was the fulcrum placed when you had to apply the most force? The least force?

____

____

2. On a sheet of paper, calculate the mechanical advantage of the three levers. Use this formula.

$$MA = \frac{\text{effort arm}}{\text{resistance arm}}$$

____

3. Which setup showed the greatest mechanical advantage? The least?

____

____

4. How do the mechanical advantages you calculated in step 3 compare to your answers to question 1?

____

____

____

5. How does the position of the fulcrum affect a lever's mechanical advantage?

____

____

Name Date Period

Chapter 8

Lab Manual 31

Exploring Pulleys

Purpose: To investigate how pulleys affect work

Materials: masking tape
2 meter sticks
2 chairs
3 pulleys
string
50-g mass
10-g mass
spring scale

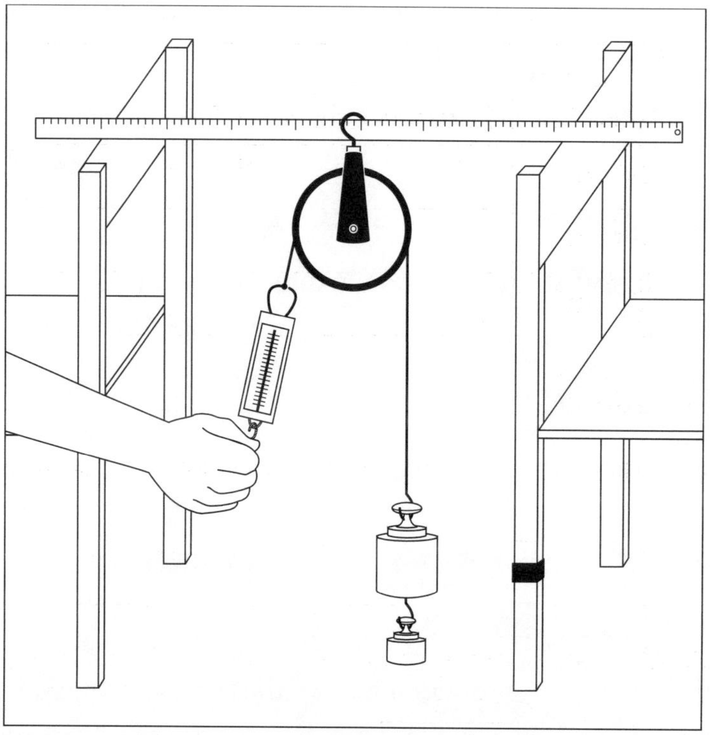

Procedure

1. Use the table below to record your data.

	Force	Distance
1 pulley		
2 pulleys		
3 pulleys		

2. Place a piece of masking tape on the leg of one of the chairs. The tape should be 20 cm above the floor.

3. Place one meter stick across two chairs as shown in the figure above. Hook a pulley onto the meter stick.

4. Hook the 10-g mass to the 50-g mass. Attach one end of the string to the 50-g mass.

5. Feed the string through the pulley. Attach the other end of the string to the spring scale.

Exploring Pulleys, continued

6. Pull the spring scale slowly and smoothly. Pull until the masses are 20 cm above the floor. Use the piece of masking tape you placed on the chair leg as a guide to let you know when the masses are at the proper height. Notice the reading on the spring scale. This reading tells the force that is needed to pull the masses. Record the force in the first column of the data table.
7. Measure the length of string between the spring scale and the pulley. Write the information in the second column of the data table.
8. Repeat steps 5 –7, using two pulleys.
9. Repeat steps 5–7 again, using three pulleys.

Questions

1. How much force was required to lift the masses, using one pulley?

____

2. How much force was required to lift the weights, using two pulleys?

____

3. What rule can you make up that involves mass, force, and the number of pulleys?

____

____

4. How far did you pull the scale, using one pulley?

____

5. How far did you pull the scale, using three pulleys?

____

6. What rule can you make up that involves distance, force, and the number of pulleys?

____

____

Name Date Period

Exploring an Inclined Plane

Purpose: To investigate how an inclined plane affects work

Materials: skateboard
spring scale
string
board, 2-m long
meter stick

Procedure

1. Use the table below to record your data.

	Force	Distance
without inclined plane		
with inclined plane		

2. Work with a partner. Use the string to attach the skateboard to the spring scale.

3. Lean the board against the desk. It should be at about a 45-degree angle. The slanted board is an inclined plane. Place the skateboard on the bottom of the board. One partner should slowly raise the spring scale up the board until the skateboard is even with the top of the desk. (You may have to stand on your desk to do this.) The other partner should read the scale. The reading on the spring scale tells the force used. Write the force in the first column of the data table.

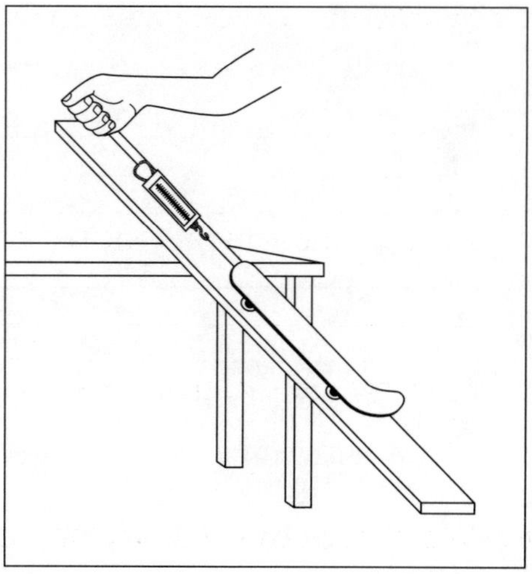

Exploring an Inclined Plane, continued

4. Place the skateboard on the floor next to your desk. One partner should slowly raise the spring scale until the skateboard is even with the top of the desk. The other partner should read the scale. Write the reading in the first column of the data table.

5. Measure the distance from the floor to the desk top. Then measure the length of the board from the floor to the desk top. Use this information to complete the data table.

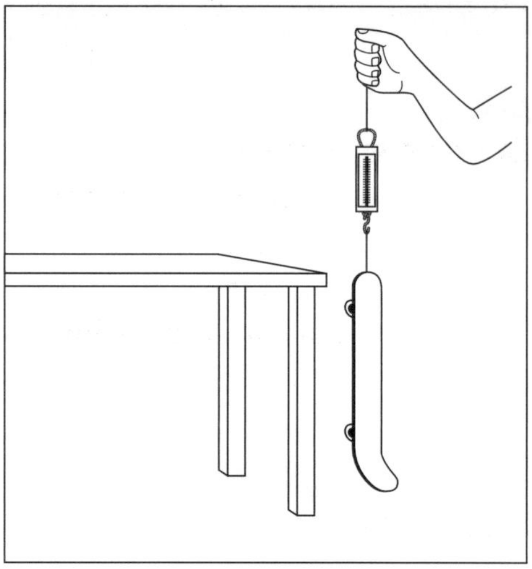

Questions

1. How did using an inclined plane affect the amount of force needed to raise the skateboard?

____

____

____

2. How did the inclined plane affect the distance the skateboard traveled?

____

____

____

Exploring Heat and the Motion of Particles

Purpose: To observe evidence that water particles move and to investigate how heat affects that motion

Materials: 3 beakers
room-temperature water
ice cube
hot water
dark food coloring
dropper
lock

Procedure

1. Use the table below to record your data.

Beaker	Observations
A	
B	
C	

2. Label the beakers *A*, *B*, and *C*.

3. Pour 250 mL of room-temperature water into beaker A. Place the ice cube in the water. Wait 3 minutes.

4. Pour 250 mL of room-temperature water into beaker B.

5. Pour 250 mL of hot water into beaker C.

Exploring Heat and the Motion of Particles, continued

6. Take the ice cube out of beaker A.
7. As soon as the water has stopped moving in all three beakers, place 1 drop of food coloring in the middle of each beaker. Wait 3 minutes.
8. Observe all 3 beakers. Write your observations in the data table.

Questions

1. What did you observe happening in each of the beakers?

____

____

____

2. Based on what you observed in this activity, do you think the particles of water are still or moving? Explain.

____

____

____

____

3. How does heat affect the motion of the particles?

____

____

____

Name Date Period

Chapter 9

Lab Manual 34

9-1 Observing and Comparing Expansion and Contraction

Use with Investigation 9-1, pages 217–218

Purpose: To observe and compare expansion and contraction of gases

	Changes in balloon
in warm water	
in cold water	
at room temperature	

Questions

1. What happened to the balloon when the flask was heated?

2. What happened to the balloon as the flask cooled?

3. What caused the changes you observed in the balloon?

Name Date Period

Exploring Heat Absorption

Purpose: To investigate how color affects the way objects absorb heat

Materials:
2 empty frozen juice cans
black construction paper
white construction paper
scissors
tape
water
black cardboard
white cardboard
2 thermometers
sunlight or 2 lamps with 100-watt bulbs

Procedure

1. Use the table below to record your data.

Time	Black can	White can
beginning		
3 minutes		
6 minutes		
9 minutes		
12 minutes		
15 minutes		
18 minutes		
21 minutes		

2. Cover one of the cans with black paper, as shown in the figure on the next page. Cover the other can with white paper.

3. Fill both of the cans with water.

4. Cut a square of black paper large enough to cover the top of the black can. Carefully poke a hole in the middle of the square. Insert a thermometer through the hole. Place the square over the top of the black can. The bottom of the thermometer should be in the center of the can.

Exploring Heat Absorption, continued

5. Repeat step 4, using the white cardboard and the white can.

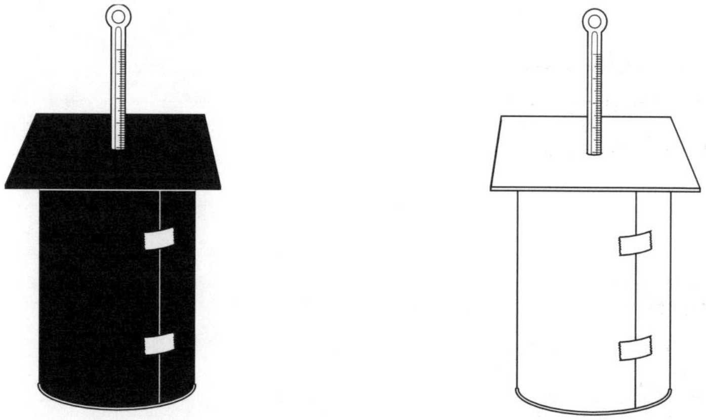

6. Place the cans in strong sunlight. If that's not possible, place a lamp with a 100-watt light bulb next to each can. The light should be shining directly on the cans. The bulbs should be as close to the cans as possible.

7. Read the temperature of the water in each can. Write the information in the data table.

8. Repeat step 7 every 3 minutes.

Questions

1. What is the source of energy that heats the cans?

____

2. Which can absorbed more heat?

____

3. How does color affect how an object absorbs heat?

____

____

4. Why would a person stay cooler in summer by wearing light-colored clothing?

____

____

____

9-2 Measuring the Rate of Heat Loss

Use with Investigation 9-2, pages 229–230

Purpose: To measure the cooling rates of different volumes of water

	Temperature (°C)	
Time	**Large jar**	**Small jar**
0 minutes		
1 minute		
2 minutes		
3 minutes		
4 minutes		
5 minutes		
6 minutes		
7 minutes		
8 minutes		
9 minutes		
10 minutes		
11 minutes		
12 minutes		
13 minutes		
14 minutes		
15 minutes		

Questions

1. What was the temperature of the water in each jar the first time you measured it? After 8 minutes? After 15 minutes?

____

2. How did the amount of water in the jar affect how fast the temperature of the water dropped?

____

____

3. What happened to the heat from the water as the water cooled?

____

Making Musical Sounds

Purpose: To produce the notes of the musical scale

Materials: 8 empty 16-oz glass bottles
masking tape
water
graduated cylinder

Procedure

1. Use the table below to record your data.

Bottle	What the sound is like
1	
2	

2. Label each bottle with a number from 1 to 8.
3. Put no water in bottle 1. In bottle 2, put 93 mL of water.
4. Blow across the opening of the bottle to produce a musical sound. Write a description of this sound in the data table.
5. Add 151 mL of water to bottle 3. Blow across the opening to produce a musical sound. How does this sound compare with the sound produced by bottle 2? Record your observations in the data table.
6. Fill the remaining bottles with the amount of water shown in the table to the right.
7. Blow across the opening of each bottle to produce a tone of the musical scale. Each bottle will produce a different note of the scale. You may need to practice to obtain good results.
8. You can change the pitch of the notes by adding or removing water from the bottle. Adjust the amount of water in each bottle until the sounds you make with the bottles resemble a musical scale.

Bottle Number	Amount of Water (mL)
1	none
2	93
3	151
4	215
5	277
6	315
7	348
8	374

Making Musical Sounds, continued

9. Try playing the following familiar tunes by blowing across the numbered bottle. The *R* indicates a rest between notes.

Tune A														
1	1	5	5	6	6	5	R	4	4	3	3	2	2	1
Tune B														
8	8	5	5	3	3	1	1	5	4	3	2	1		

Questions

1. What is the name of Tune A?

2. What is the name of Tune B?

3. To make the pitch of the bottle higher, what must you do?

4. To make the pitch of the bottle lower, what must you do?

10-1

Inferring How Sound Waves Travel

Use with Investigation 10-1, pages 252–253

Purpose: To demonstrate that sound waves are vibrations that travel through matter

How the rubber band was plucked	Observations

Questions

1. In Step 7, what happened to the salt when you plucked the rubber band?

2. What do you think caused the salt to move? Explain.

3. In Step 8, how did the force you used to pluck the rubber band affect the sound it made?

4. In Step 8, how did the force you used to pluck the rubber band affect the salt on the plastic wrap?

Name Date Period

Making a Pinhole Camera

Purpose: To build a pinhole camera

Materials: empty oatmeal box
waxed paper
rubber band
pin

Procedure

1. Use the table below to record your data.

	Observations	
Object pointed at	**With small hole**	**With large hole**

2. Take the lid off the oatmeal box. Spread the waxed paper over the opening of the box. The waxed paper should be tight and smooth. Hold the waxed paper in place with the rubber band, as shown in the figure above.

3. Use the pin to poke a hole in the bottom of the oatmeal box. The hole should be in the center of the bottom of the box.

4. To use your pinhole camera, point the bottom of the box at a brightly lit object. Look at the waxed paper. How good is the image you see? Record your observations in the data table. What is the position of the image? Record your observations.

Making a Pinhole Camera, continued

5. Repeat step 4 with at least 4 more bright objects.
6. Make the hole in your pinhole camera a little bigger. How does that change the image? Keep making the hole a little bigger and checking the image. Record your observations in the data table.

Questions

1. How are the real objects different from their images in the camera?

____

____

2. How could you increase the quality of the images?

____

____

3. What happens to the image as the hole gets bigger?

____

____

Explore Further

What happens if you use different sizes and kinds of containers or different materials in place of the waxed paper? Make another camera from some of these materials and find out.

Name Date Period

Chapter 10
Lab Manual
40

10-2 Measuring Angles of Reflected Rays

Use with Investigation 10-2, pages 262–263

Purpose: To measure angles at which a light ray hits and is reflected from a mirror

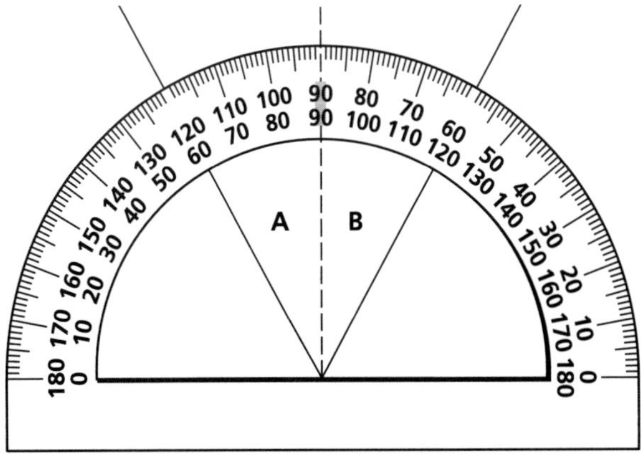

Trial	Angle A	Angle B
1		
2		
3		

Questions

1. Which angle—A or B—shows the angle at which the light traveled to the mirror?

____

2. Which angle shows the angle at which the light was reflected from the mirror?

____

3. How do angles A and B compare?

____

____

Exploring Electric Charges

Purpose: To observe how an electric charge affects the way an object behaves

Materials: meter stick
masking tape
2 balloons
string
wool cloth

Procedure

1. Use the table below to record your data.

Steps	Objects	What I think will happen	What happened
5–6			
7–8			
9			
10–11			

2. Tape the meter stick to the top of your desk. Make sure it extends over the edge.
3. Blow up one of the balloons. Tie the end of the balloon shut. Attach one end of the string to the balloon. Use the other end of the string to hang the balloon from the meter stick.
4. Hold the piece of wool cloth away from the balloon.
5. What do you think will happen if you move the wool toward the balloon? Record your prediction in the data table.
6. Slowly move the wool cloth close to the balloon. Observe what happens. Write your observations in the data table.

Exploring Electric Charges, continued

7. Rub the balloon with the wool cloth for 30 seconds. Move the wool cloth away from the balloon. What do you think will happen if you move the cloth toward the balloon? Record your prediction in the data table.
8. Slowly move the wool cloth toward the balloon. Observe what happens. Write your observations in the data table.
9. Blow up the second balloon. Move it toward the first balloon. Observe what happens. Record you observations.
10. Rub the second balloon with the wool cloth. What do you think will happen if you move this balloon toward the first balloon? Record you prediction.
11. Hold the second balloon away from the first balloon. Move the second balloon slowly toward the first balloon. Observe what happens. Write your observations in the data table.

Questions

1. Did the wool cloth or the balloons have a charge before they were rubbed together? How do you know?

____

____

2. Did the balloons and the cloth have a charge after they were rubbed together? How do you know?

____

____

3. How did the balloon and the wool cloth affect each other after they were rubbed together? What does this tell about the charge on each object?

____

____

4. How did the two balloons affect each other after they were rubbed? What does this tell you about the charge on the balloons?

____

____

Identifying Electric Conductors

Purpose: To explore how well various solutions conduct electricity

Materials:
- 8 paper cups
- graduated cylinder
- spoon
- salt
- mineral oil
- rubbing alcohol
- dry cell battery
- 3 wires with insulation removed from the ends
- water
- baking soda
- 4 drinking straws
- sugar
- orange juice
- vinegar
- light bulb and holder
- 2 nails

Procedure

1. Use the table below to record your data.

Material	Prediction	Observation	Conductor or Nonconductor
baking soda			
salt			
sugar			
mineral oil			
orange juice			
rubbing alcohol			
vinegar			
plain water			
other			

2. For each of the materials in the table, predict whether it is a conductor or a nonconductor. Write your prediction in the data table.
3. Pour 125 mL of water into each of 4 cups.
4. Pour 1/2 spoonful of baking soda into one of the cups of water. Stir with a drinking straw until the baking soda dissolves.

Identifying Electric Conductors, continued

5. Repeat step 4 with the salt.
6. Repeat step 4 with the sugar.
7. Pour the orange juice, mineral oil, rubbing alcohol, and vinegar into the remaining cups. One liquid should go in each cup.
8. Attach one end of a wire to one battery terminal and the other end to the lamp terminal, as shown in the figure. Attach one end of the second wire to the bulb holder. Wrap the loose end around a nail. Attach one end of the third wire to a battery terminal. Wrap the loose end around the other nail.
9. Dip the two nails into the liquid in the cup with the baking soda. Make sure the nails don't touch each other. Observe what happens to the light bulb. Record your observations in the data table.
10. Repeat step 9, using each of the remaining cups.

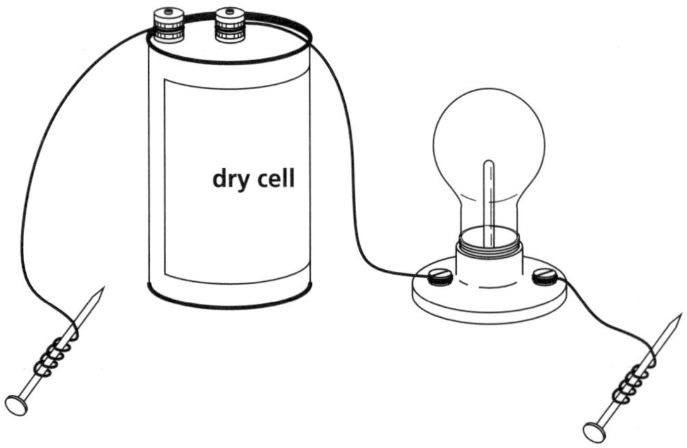

Questions

1. If the light bulb glows brightly, the material is a good conductor. If the light bulb glows faintly, the material is a poor conductor. If the light bulb does not glow at all, the material is a nonconductor. Complete the data table by telling whether each material is a good conductor, or a nonconductor.
2. How do your predictions about which materials are conductors compare to the actual results?

   ____

   ____
3. Which material made the light shine the brightest?

   ____

11-1 Constructing Series Circuits

Use with Investigation 11-1, pages 290–291

Purpose: To construct and study a series circuit

Circuit	Schematic diagram	Prediction	Observations
A			
B			
C			

Questions

1. What items make up circuit A? What kind of circuit is it?

____

____

2. What items make up circuit B? What kind of circuit is it?

____

____

Constructing Series Circuits, continued

3. How brightly did the bulbs in circuit B shine compared to the bulb in circuit A? Explain.

____

____

____

4. What happened in circuit B when one of the bulbs was unscrewed? Why did that happen?

____

____

5. How brightly did the bulbs in circuit C shine compared to the bulbs in circuit B? Explain.

____

____

____

Name Date Period

11-2 Constructing Parallel Circuits

Use with Investigation 11-2, pages 295–296

Purpose: To construct and study parallel circuits

Circuit	Schematic diagram	Prediction	Observations
A			
B			
C			
D			
E			

Constructing Parallel Circuits, continued

Questions

1. What items make up circuit C? What kind of circuit is it?

2. Are the cells in circuit D connected in series or in parallel?

3. Are the cells in circuit E connected in series or in parallel?

4. What happened in circuit A when one of the bulbs was unscrewed? Why?

5. How brightly did the bulbs in circuit B shine compared to the bulbs in circuit A? Why?

6. What happened in circuit B when various bulbs were unscrewed? Why?

7. What happened in circuit C when various bulbs were unscrewed? Why?

8. How brightly did the bulbs in circuit D shine compared to the bulbs in circuit A? Why?

9. How brightly did the bulbs in circuit E shine compared to the bulbs in circuit D? Why?

Exploring Magnetism

Purpose: To determine what materials can block a magnetic field

Materials:
- support stand
- rod
- thread
- metric ruler
- copper sheet
- aluminum foil
- plywood
- clamp
- bar magnet
- paper clip
- sheet of paper
- cotton fabric
- plastic wrap

Procedure

1. Use the table below to record your data.

Material	Does it block a magnetic field?
sheet of paper	
copper sheet	
cotton fabric	
aluminum foil	
plastic wrap	
plywood	

2. Clamp the rod onto the support stand.

3. Place the bar magnet on the desk top some distance from the support stand, as shown in the figure.

4. Tie one end of the thread around the paper clip. Tie the other end to the rod. Make sure that the paper clip is attracted to the bar magnet. Tighten the thread to leave a 3-cm gap between the paper clip and the magnet.

Exploring Magnetism, continued

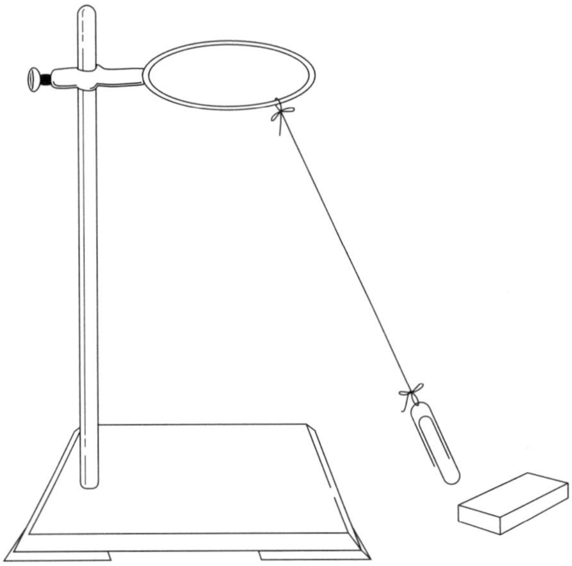

5. Place the sheet of paper between the magnet and the paper clip. If the material blocks the magnetic field, the paper clip will hang straight down. Record your observations in the data table.
6. Repeat step 5, using each of the remaining materials.
7. Repeat step 5 again, using two other materials you choose.

Questions

1. Which materials blocked the magnetic field?

____

____

____

2. What rule can you make up about blocking a magnetic field?

____

____

____

Name Date Period

Chapter 12

Lab Manual

46

12-1

Observing Magnetic Lines of Force

Use with Investigation 12-1, pages 308–309

Purpose: To observe the lines of force around magnets

Part	Bar magnet	Horseshoe magnet
A		
B		
C		

Questions

1. Describe the pattern made by the lines of force of the single bar magnet.

2. In Part B, did the poles of the bar magnets attract or repel each other? How did the lines of force show this?

3. In Part C, did the poles of the bar magnets attract or repel each other? How do you know?

4. How were the patterns on the bar magnet similar to those on the horseshoe magnet?

Experimenting With a Compass

Purpose: To make a compass and to determine what materials will affect it

Materials:

needle
small piece of sponge
tray
magnetic compass
iron nail
steel paper clip
bar magnet
correction fluid
water
crumpled paper ball
wooden pencil
eraser

Procedure

1. Use the table below to record your data.

Material	Does it affect the compass?
paper ball	
iron nail	
wooden pencil	
paper clip	
eraser	

2. Rub one end of the bar magnet along the needle. Rub it in the same direction 25 times.

3. Find an object in the classroom that is attracted to the magnet. Use this object to test the needle. The object should be attracted to the needle, too. If the needle does not attract the object, repeat step 2.

4. Slide the needle through the sponge so that it sticks out on each end. Use the correction fluid to paint one end of the needle white.

5. Fill the tray with water. Float the sponge in the water. Keep the bar magnet away from the needle. If it floats freely, one end of the needle should point toward Earth's magnetic north pole. Use a compass to check your magnet.

Experimenting With a Compass, continued

6. Gently spin the sponge. Observe what happens.
7. Move the crumpled paper around near the needle. Record your observations in the data table.
8. Repeat step 5, using each of the other materials.
9. Repeat step 5 again, using two materials you choose.

Questions

1. In step 6, what happened to the needle after you spun it?

____

____

2. Why do you think this happened?

____

____

3. Which materials affected the compass?

____

____

4. Which materials did not affect the compass?

____

____

Explore Further

Use your compass to give directions to a particular place.

Name ______________________ Date ____________ Period ____________

12-2 Constructing an Electromagnet

Use with Investigation 12-2, pages 319–320

Purpose: To demonstrate how to increase the magnetic properties of an electromagnet

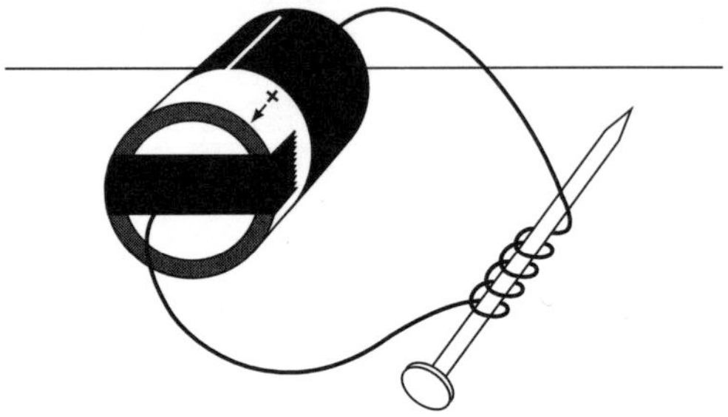

Number of turns of wire coil	Number of paper clips
5	
10	
15	
25	

Questions

1. In step 6, what happened to the paper clips when you removed one end of the wire from the battery?

____

2. How did the number of coils in the wire affect the electromagnet?

____

____